all color book of
KITTENS

Howard Loxton

octopus Octopus Books

First published 1974 by
Octopus Books Limited
59 Grosvenor Street, London W1

ISBN 0 7064 0325 8

© 1974 Octopus Books Limited

Produced by Mandarin Publishers Limited
14 Westlands Road, Quarry Bay, Hong Kong

Printed in Hong Kong

Contents

You and your kitten

The Cat is one of the best mothers in the animal world and a kitten is probably one of the most appealing young creatures you will ever see. Born into the world defenceless, hungry and blind, kittens soon develop sturdy and independent characters of their own. Until their eyes open, on about the ninth day after birth, they will do no more than sleep and suckle, and should be left quietly to their mother's care in a warm but airy place out of draughts and full sunlight. As soon as they can take their first stumbling steps away from the nest, their inquisitive natures will lead them to explore their immediate environment, with frequent dashes back to the comforting security of their mother.

The mother cat does a much better job at training her kittens than any human foster parent could do, teaching them to wash themselves and instilling strict toilet discipline so that they will grow up with fastidious habits. The date at which kittens can be weaned will vary according to the size of the litter and the mother's supply of milk, but will usually be about three to four weeks after birth. The mother will probably begin to discourage the kittens from feeding from her and allow them to show interest in her own food but you can encourage the transition by offering a little milk enriched with glucose, first on the tip of your finger, then in a saucer. Later baby ceral or creamed rice with evaporated milk can be given. At six weeks most kittens will be fully weaned, but they should not be taken from their mother until they are at least that old and preferably older, although there is no reason why you should not choose your kitten when it is younger.

Choosing a kitten

If you are fortunate enough to be able to visit a breeder more than once and watch a litter develop before you decide which kitten to have, you will be able both to judge the health and the qualities of the whole family and to see the way in which the individual characters of the kittens develop.

Naturally, not everyone gets a kitten from a professional breeder. You may have a friend or neighbour whose cat has kittened or you may simply be 'adopted' by a stray, but if you want a pedigree cat it is wise to go to a reputable breeder. Although any well cared for cat will make a delightful companion, different breeds vary in character and in the demands they make. Long-haired cats, for example, will always require a great deal of grooming, and the oriental types will expect much more of your time and attention.

Unless you are prepared for a great deal of trouble, expense and possible unhappiness it is best to control the flood of sympathy natural to any cat lover for a particularly unhappy, scruffy little kitten crouching in the corner of a pet shop window. However, if you still feel bound to save the poor creature, think hard about what you are taking on.

In any litter of kittens you will usually find one that appears to be the leader. Such a kitten will not necessarily grow up to be stronger and healthier than its siblings, but its dominance is a good indication that it is starting off a strong and healthy kitten. If you are primarily looking for a cat which will be an affectionate companion, however, it is probably better to avoid this leader kitten, for he (or she, for it will not necessarily be a male) may prove to be a bossy and self-willed adult.

Kittens are naturally gregarious, and a kitten which avoids its brothers and sisters and hides away on its own may have something wrong with it. If you are attracted to a weaker or more helpless-looking kitten, be sure you take a close and careful look at it before you make up your mind. However, the weaker kitten of a litter, if basically sound in health, will quite probably grow up into a strong cat and often proves to be more intelligent than its tougher siblings.

You can learn a lot simply by observing the kittens' behaviour with one another and with their mother, but try pulling a piece of string across the floor and you will soon see which kittens give the liveliest response. The leader will not necessarily be the one with the quickest reactions.

If there are any signs of runny eyes, dirty ears or diarrhoea among the litter you may be wise to reject them all. No good breeder will mind you making a careful inspection of his kittens; often he will warn you beforehand if there is anything wrong. In such a case he will probably suggest that the kittens will not be available until the vet has given them a clear bill of health. If you still have any doubts you can always arrange with the breeder to return the kitten if your own vet finds any trouble.

If you are buying a pedigree kitten, the breeder should give you a copy of the pedigree and, if the kitten is old enough to have had its vaccinations, a form stating when the injections

were given. If you wish to show the cat, it will be necessary to register it with the appropriate authority, which also records any change of ownership.

When you first take the kitten home it will be lonely and disorientated away from its family, so make sure that you can spend plenty of time with it during the first few days in its new surroundings. If during the week you are away at work all day, it is essential to collect it at the weekend so that you can be at home with it for as long as possible. In fact, if it is going to be left alone a great deal it would be much better to have two cats so that they can keep each other company — a young kitten will not be happy on its own.

Cat carriers

Do not try to carry the kitten home in your arms or tucked into your coat. A little kitten, easily frightened, may succeed in wriggling out of your grasp and become lost or hurt. To carry it you need a container in which the cat can be comfortable, warm and can breathe easily. Animal welfare societies often sell inexpensive and well-designed cardboard carriers. These have the advantage of being disposable, and can be burned if they have carried an infected cat, but you will probably prefer to buy a proper cat basket which you can use whenever travelling with the cat. Wicker baskets are traditional — they are lightweight, airy and allow the cat to see what is going on all around them. Fibreglass carriers are heavier and usually have only one opening through which the cat can see, but they are easier to disinfect if necessary. Whatever carrier you use, line it with a few layers of

newspaper and a warm blanket. If it is very cold and you are going to be in the open air, a hot water bottle beneath the blanket may make the kitten more comfortable.

Cats are normally good travellers, taking a lively interest in the passing scene or curling up and going to sleep according to their fancy. But if you are driving, and particularly if you have no other passengers in the car, keep the kitten in its container or it may distract you and cause an accident.

Equipment

Before you collect your kitten you must make all the necessary preparations for its reception. A shallow circular basket can make a cosy place for a kitten to curl up in and newspaper makes an excellent bedding which is easy to replace. You can make or buy such a cat bed, and there are many kinds sold in pet shops, but more cats prefer to choose a place of their own to sleep. Do not be surprised if the kitten decides to settle down somewhere quite different, though if it is somewhere you do not wish it to use habitually, it must be gently discouraged.

The litter tray

You will need a litter tray, at least until the cat is old enough to be let out into your garden, and it will be a permanent necessity for a house-bound or apartment cat. The tray must be large enough for a cat to sit inside it and should be shallow enough to allow the kitten to climb into it or to allow a larger

be torn to ribbons it is advisable to provide a special scratching place. All cats need to 'sharpen' their claws: in fact they are not actually sharpening them but are exercising their muscles and removing the worn-out sheaths on their front claws to reveal the new, sharp claws beneath. You may decide upon an unimportant chair which you do not mind having ruined, but it is much better to make a special scratching post. Pet shops sell specially-made posts, but a rough (not splintery) log or an old rug wrapped around a piece of wood will serve very well.

Feeding and grooming equipment

It is a good idea to keep the food and water dishes you use for your cat separate from those used by your family, but there is no need to buy special pet bowls provided you use ones which will not spill easily, for small kittens will soon knock them over. You may find it useful to put food dishes down on a tray to make it easier to clear up any mess.

You should also equip yourself with a brush and comb for grooming and, if your cat is to stay indoors and is a breed such as a Siamese which grows long claws, you will need a pair of nail clippers. If your cat goes out, it can wear down its claws on hard outdoor surfaces, and clippers are not necessary.

Medical check-up

However you obtain your kitten it is a good idea to take it to a veterinarian for a check up as soon as possible, particularly if you have obtained it from a pet shop or other source and cannot be sure that it comes from healthy stock and a good home. The vet will make sure that there is nothing wrong with the kitten and will tell you how and when to treat it for fleas, mites and worms. These parasites are all very prevalent among young kittens and cannot always be avoided even in the most carefully run catteries. You can also make arrangements for the kitten to be given inoculations against feline enteritis as soon as it is old enough.

cat to perch on the edge. It must also be deep enough to prevent the cat litter being scattered all over the floor — although with some cats that seems to be a hopeless wish. Cats naturally bury their droppings and your pet will go through all the motions of doing so in its tray. There are some pet owners who consider that a few layers of newspaper make an adequate absorption pad in the litter tray, while others will use deep layers of peat. The simplest and most convenient arrangement is to line the tray with a layer or two of newspaper, to prevent the wet litter sticking to the tray, and then to scatter a shallow layer of proprietary cat litter which is made to absorb both moisture and smell. This is not cheap but it will make much less mess than using sand or ashes. Remember to remove solid lumps and to change the litter frequently or you may find the kitten using a different place to draw attention to the dirty state of its tray.

Scratching posts

Unless you want your furniture, carpets and wall coverings to

Settling in

Your kitten will be nervous and a little frightened of its new surroundings until it has fully explored them, so try to avoid a lot of noise and visitors until it has really settled in. If you have children, warn them that they must be very quiet and gentle with the new member of the household. It is probably best to take the kitten home when the children are out of the house. Make sure that it cannot come to any obvious harm by placing a guard before open fires and keeping an eye on landings and stairs from which it might fall, but let it investigate its new home at its leisure.

Show the kitten its litter tray and perhaps scratch in the litter a little until the kitten understands what it is for. After the journey the kitten may need it badly. It helps the kitten to know what is expected if, at least to begin with, you use the kind of litter it has been used to previously; you can make a change when the kitten has learned where to go.

A nervous kitten will not have much appetite and will probably not show any sign of being hungry until it has explored its surroundings and has satisfied itself there is no hidden danger. Have ready a small amount of the food it is used to, and offer it a little slightly warmed milk to give it encouragement. When your kitten sits down and starts to wash itself you will know that it has decided that it is safe.

Feeding

Before you collect your kitten you should ask the breeder what sort of food it has been used to so that you can give it the same. If you keep to its familiar food at first, you can begin to vary the kitten's diet to suit your personal circumstances when it is happily settled in. Remember that a kitten needs frequent meals of small quantity, for its stomach is very small — it is only the size of a walnut — and cannot cope with much at one time. It is popularly believed that cats never eat more than is good for them, but this is just not true, and overeating will lead to indigestion just as readily as it does in human beings.

There is endless argument over what foods are suitable for cats and kittens and whether they should be served cooked or raw. What you give your kitten will depend on what you can afford and what you can readily obtain, but it is essential that you provide a balanced and varied diet. If food is totally ignored or much of it left do not leave it down to attract dirt and flies. Throw it away and put fresh food down at the next mealtime. Young kittens are not usually too choosy in what they are prepared to eat, but if you find that as they get older they refuse what you offer unless it be some particular delicacy they have acquired a taste for, you will have to be tough and insist they eat the food they are given or starve. If they do not immediately give in to them, they will probably return to the food and eat it quite happily. However, it is not advisable to place bets on the outcome of this battle of wills — there is certainly no guarantee that you will win.

At six weeks old, which is the earliest you should ever take a kitten from its mother, it will need four to five small meals a day. Two should be meat or fish, the others can be milk-based meals. It will probably enjoy a little baby ceral or creamed rice mixed with evaporated milk — cow's milk does not agree with some cats and gives them diarrhoea. Finely minced beef, cooked and boned fish, raw egg yolk or scrambled eggs should all prove acceptable and later, other kinds of meat, offal, chicken and rabbit can be introduced. Always cook meat such as pork which might harbour parasites, making sure it is well done just as you would for human beings, and always cook fish unless it is really fresh. Cats are carnivores and will eat raw meat in the wild, but such food is always freshly killed. Be careful that there are no small bones or splintery bones which could lodge in the kitten's throat or pierce its mouth or stomach. Even when your cat is older you should be very careful about bones, for although a wild cat will cope with all the bones of a carcass, cooking makes bones brittle and there is no point in taking risks. Bones should always be removed from fish and cooked meat, but many cats will enjoy having a large raw beef bone to gnaw on, especially when they are teething.

Canned cat foods can be introduced when the kitten has

settled down and is eating happily, but they are often very rich and should be given sparingly to young kittens. Even when a cat is adult you should never rely on them exclusively. There are also a number of extremely convenient dry foods on the market which can be given when the cat gets older. Water should always be available. Even if your cat likes milk — and contrary to accepted belief many do not — remember that it is a·food and that fresh drinking water will still be needed.

If your kitten does not have a garden to play in where it can eat a little grass, you should keep a pot of grass growing indoors for it to nibble occasionally. Cats should always have access to grass, which they use as a natural emetic to help them disgorge the fur they swallow in washing themselves and to correct other small disorders.

Training and discipline

Never fuss a new kitten but give it plenty of attention. Talk to it often in a gentle and reassuring way. Encourage it to explore the house with you, for you must now provide the security and confidence it previously got from its mother. Always allow it to climb on to your lap or snuggle against your shoulder. Stroke it very gently with one finger, especially on top of the head — but never hold on to it against its will.

Play with your kitten when it wants to play, but do not try and get it to go on playing if it does not want to. Kittens tire very easily and need a great deal of rest. One minute they will be rushing around all over the place and the next minute they will be sound asleep.

Never smack or scold a tiny kitten or you will make it nervous. Every household will have a different set of prohibitions for its pets, but if you want to train a kitten not to do something, tap it gently on the nose and quietly but firmly say no. If it digs its claws into you, remove them (a little kitten cannot do you much harm) and tap them gently. A well-trained cat will soon respond to your voice alone. It is often suggested that a rolled-up newspaper can be used to smack a cat or to bang the ground or table behind it in reproof, but cats are mischievous by nature and this will only encourage them to make a game of it by seeing if they can do what is forbidden and then run away before you can reach for the newspaper!

Never permit a kitten to do something which you will forbid it to do when it has grown up. It will not understand why you have changed your mind and, thinking you grossly illogical, may prove very uncooperative. Another general rule to follow is that you can teach a cat *not to do* certain things, but it is pointless trying to teach a cat to *do* anything. A cat has a very strong will of its own: you can suggest things to it and encourage certain habits and games, but in the end the cat will be the one to decide whether to please itself or to please you.

If you already have another pet it is unwise to leave it alone with the new kitten until they have got used to each other. Once the older animal has accepted that the kitten is a permanent resident, it will usually make friends and may welcome the kitten from the start as a new playmate. The kitten may spit at first but this is only because it is instinctively on the defensive. When it finds no threat is intended, it will rapidly make friends. In the case of another cat which refuses to accept a newcomer, an odd but effective method of bringing them together is to wipe the kitten with some of the older cat's urine.

The older cat will then wash the kitten and begin to accept responsibility for it.

Diseases of cats

The two most dangerous diseases which affect cats are feline infectious enteritis, or panleukopenia, and feline distemper, also known as pneumonitis or cat flu. Panleukopenia, which is fatal in more than three-quarters of cases, and is particularly dangerous for kittens, requires immediate veterinary treatment if the kitten is to have any chance of survival. It is a viral disease and does not necessarily cause enteritis at all. There may be diarrhoea or constipation but the first symptom is usually vomiting. The kitten loses its appetite and appears to be thirsty, but although it crouches over its water bowl, it will only take a lap or two. It will look off-colour and glassy-eyed and its tail may be stretched out behind it instead of curled around in the way that cats normally sit. Fortunately there are a number of vaccines on the market which are both safe and effective. If the breeder has not supplied a certificate, properly completed by a vet, stating that the kitten has been inoculated, you must be sure that it is done, preferably when the kitten is between seven and ten weeks old.

It is thought that the vaccine for feline infectious enteritis also gives some protection against cat flu, which is the loose term for a whole group of viral diseases. As with the common cold in humans this may be caused by so many variations of virus that immunization is very difficult and there is no accepted, reliable vaccine. Sometimes the disease affects the nose, mouth and throat, sometimes it is largely centred on the lungs. Like panleukopenia it is *highly* infectious and if you suspect your kitten of having contracted it, you should keep both it and you well away from other cats. It is also a good idea to telephone the vet before taking it up to the surgery in case he wants to make special arrangements to avoid contact with other cats. The first symptom is sneezing, but of course many other things make a cat sneeze so do not jump to conclusions at the first sign of a snuffle. Sneezing is usually followed by a clear discharge from the eyes, a runny nose and a rise in temperature. The kitten may salivate excessively and cough, and will almost certainly lose its appetite.

Loss of appetite is almost always a sign of something wrong. Cats and kittens do not just decide to go on a diet. Do not, of course, be misled by a simple refusal to eat something which your kitten does not like or with which it has got bored. However, if you find that the cat continues to refuse food, then it is time for concern. All cat owners who get to know their pets will find it very easy to tell when their kitten is off-colour.

Worms

Worms, which in kittens are usually indicated by a swollen stomach, are easily treated by pills. Although worm pills are available on the market, it is much better to get them from your vet, for he will make sure that you have the right pill in the right dosage for your particular kitten. To give a kitten a pill hold it, tummy uppermost, in the crook of your arm and make it open its mouth by squeezing slightly at the sides and then holding it open with one finger (you will need quite a lot of pressure). If you are holding the pill between the index finger and thumb of the same hand you should be able to pop the pill to the back of its throat. Then hold the mouth shut and massage the throat until the kitten has swallowed the pill. Don't put the kitten down or let it run away until you are quite sure that the pill *has* been swallowed. If it wants to be difficult, a cat can very determinedly hold a pill in its mouth and spit it out later when you're not looking. Of course, if you can get someone else to hold the kitten you will find the task much easier.

Fleas and mites

Fleas and mites can be another source of trouble, but they too are easily treated if dealt with in time. Frequent scratching may indicate the presence of fleas. A badly infested kitten will need dusting with flea powder, but make sure that it really is suitable for cats. Shops have been known to sell flea powders to cat owners which on close inspection have been labelled 'Not to be used on cats'. DDT and DDT-based powders should never be used, but Pyrethrum is harmless to cats. Dust both the kitten and its quarters. If you are lucky and there really are only one or two fleas you may be nimble enough to pick them off and kill them.

Mites, which infest the ear, cause ear canker or otodetic mange. If your kitten is constantly scratching and shaking its head this is a sign they may be present and you will usually also find a secretion of fluid in the ear. Your vet will give you drops to kill the mites, and you will have to clean out the ear with cotton buds on a stick. Because too strong an antidote may cause damage to the kitten, this may be quite an extended procedure involving frequent treatments with small doses. Your vet will tell you how many drops to use and how often to apply them. Such a condition should never be ignored for it may lead to secondary infection and serious damage to the kitten's ear.

There are a number of other small parasites which are fortunately less common, but if your kitten shows signs of skin irritation, bare patches or anything suspicious, don't take risks – take it to the vet. No vet will mind the occasional false alarm, but he will be very concerned if an illness is allowed to develop, ignored and unchecked.

Naturally, all poisons and dangerous things should be locked up well out of a kitten's way, but if you find that a cat has licked up some spilt weed-killer or you suspect that something has poisoned it, it is useful to have some 'universal antidote' in your medicine cupboard. This can be made up from two parts of powdered charcoal (burnt toast will do if you have to make some up in an emergency), one part milk of magnesia and one part tannic acid or strong tea. It can't do the kitten any harm, so try to get a couple of spoonfuls down its throat (more, of course, for an adult cat). This antidote is capable of absorbing up to fifteen times its own weight in coal-tar poison and more than a hundred times its weight in strychnine! Next, telephone the vet and tell him what you think the kitten has eaten. He will either advise you on what more you can do, or ask you to bring the kitten along with the suspected poison so that he can decide on the antidote.

Bowel disorders

Constipation in kittens can be eased by gently inserting a greased toothpick about a quarter of an inch into the rectum and by administering a little medicinal paraffin. Sometimes constipation may be caused by a ball of fur which is blocking the rectum – one of the disorders which can normally be avoided by always making sure there is grass available for the kitten to eat. Looseness can be put right by mixing a little kaolin powder with the kitten's usual food. Both conditions, however, may be the result of a change of diet and should not cause you too much concern. However, if they persist for more than twenty-four hours or if the animal seems to be in pain you should consult your vet.

Collars and leads

If you want your kitten to wear a collar, which it obviously must if it is to carry an identity disc, you should get it used to the idea very gradually by putting the collar on for a short period each day. Never, however, introduce the collar after the kitten has done something wrong, for then it will seem like a punishment. Cats that make it quite clear they hate wearing a collar should not be forced to wear one; others will show them off with pride. Every cat will protest a little at first at feeling something strange around its neck, but most will rapidly get used to it. Make sure that the collar has an elastic section which can stretch to allow the cat to free itself if the collar should

catch on the branch of a tree or get hooked on something.

Some breeds, such as the Siamese, will usually take to walking on a lead if you introduce them to the idea when they are young kittens. You must first get the kitten accustomed to a collar, or you can use a body harness which has the advantage of not pulling on the neck. Let the kitten play with the lead until it gets used to it. Only when it has begun to take the lead for granted should you attempt to hold the other end. First walk the way the kitten wants to go, then pull gently on the lead and call the kitten to you. Frequent and very brief lessons should be the rule until the kitten has accepted the idea. Do not be too disappointed if the attempt fails, however, for many cats refuse ever to walk on a lead: they usually just flop firmly down and refuse to move. None the less it is worth the attempt, especially for the housebound cat, for it means that not only can you give it much-needed exercise, but you enable it to share your company and see much more of the outside world than it can through a window at home.

Neutering

If you have not already decided, you must soon make up your mind whether or not you are going to have your cat neutered. Unless you intend to breed (and you should not do this until you are experienced at looking after cats), there is very little choice, but you must think very hard about your responsibility in the matter. There are already far too many stray cats and unwanted kittens in the world and it is wrong to add to their number unnecessarily.

An un-neutered or 'entire' adult male will spray urine to mark his territories both outdoors and in. The pungent odour is unpleasant and unmistakable. Entire cats living in the country-side can reasonably expect to have a territory of their own, but in most of our towns and cities there are many cats in the same area and toms constantly get involved in fights over territorial rights or over females. Even if they emerge triumphant, they may be badly battered in the process: their injuries may be serious and mean pain for them and veterinary bills for you. An entire cat will also want to spend much more time out on the prowl and consequently will spend much less time with you.

Unless you are prepared to keep a female indoors and watch her carefully so that she does not get out when in 'season' and receptive to advances from males, you will almost inevitably end up with a litter of kittens. If you are prepared to keep them all or can guarantee to find them good homes, you will find that seeing a cat through her pregnancy and helping her rear her kittens can be a delightful and rewarding experience, but if you cannot undertake that responsibility then it is a risk that you should not accept.

Breeding

Cats are officially considered to be kittens for cat show purposes up to the age of nine months. They will, of course, go on growing long after that, but many females will have reached sexual maturity much earlier. If you do decide to wait and let your cat have kittens of her own try to avoid letting her mate the first time that she comes on call. Wait until she is older and more able to deal with motherhood. If you have a pedigree cat it is wise to find a sire which will enhance the good points of your own pet. You will be able to find the name of the owner of a suitable stud cat from the appropriate breed society or from the breeder from whom you obtained your kitten in the first place.

Most female cats can cope instinctively with motherhood, but there is the rare mother cat who will ignore or reject her kittens. Under even more tragic circumstances, a litter may be left motherless. In both cases the kittens have to be hand reared. This can be a very demanding process since you must replace the mother in tending to all the kittens' needs — not only feeding — cleaning them, helping them to excrete — everything — and it is exhausting and time consuming. The possibility of having to rear a litter yourself is remote, but if you are prepared to allow your cat to have a litter at all, you must be prepared to accept this responsibility too.

Of course, kittens grow up. No animal can remain a baby forever and, sadly, some people neglect their kittens when they reach maturity and no longer seem quite so winsome. An animal is not a plaything and should never be treated as such. People who lose interest in their cats when the novelty and charm of kittenhood turn into the beauty and grace of the grown animal should never own a pet. However elegant an adult cat may be, even if it has children and grandchildren, it will still be a kitten at heart, display the same vitality and often enjoy the same games. Of course an adult cat will take on an added dignity which will not allow it to tolerate the same amount of teasing and silliness that it would as a kitten, and its developed intelligence can lead to more complicated play. It will have greater patience, too, and the tendency to fall asleep in the middle of a game will disappear. It will inevitably grow less active with advancing years, but will always respond to the affection and attention that was so necessary when it was small.

Male cats are neutered by castration which is a simple operation if performed on a young cat. It can usually be undertaken from about the age of four months, but because the best time depends on the rate at which the kitten matures, the date should be decided by your vet. If the operation is carried out at under six months of age, it is so painless that it can be done without an anaesthetic, although one is often given. You will be able to take your kitten to the vet in the morning and collect it later the same day. Why not fix a provisional date for the

operation when you take the kitten for injections against feline enteritis?

Spaying a female is a more complicated operation since it involves an abdominal incision and the removal of the ovaries and uterus. Your pet will probably have to be left overnight and later taken back to have a few stitches removed. The operation is easier if done when the cat is young, about five to six months old, but it can be performed at any age if you want your kitten to grow up and have one litter of kittens first.

Neutering does not change the basic character of a cat, although having its strong urge to mate removed will tend to make the cat more settled at home. It will not seek out fights and will be less inclined to prowl about all night. This may result in less exercise and a tendency to put on weight, but remember that a fat cat is still the result of overfeeding – a neutered cat should be encouraged to play more games and its diet should be watched. It seems likely that there are one or two skin conditions to which elderly neutered males seem to be slightly more susceptible, but these are the result of old age, not of neutering.

The new arrival

Below
Newly-born kittens may be kept warm over a hot water bottle if their mother is having a difficult delivery. Most cats give birth without any problems and can cope with everything themselves, but they may welcome the presence of their owners. You should certainly be at hand if your cat is kittening and should learn what has to be done in case assistance is required.

Top right
A Blue Burmese with her litter.
Centre
A litter of very young Abyssinian kittens, their eyes not yet open.
Below
A proud Blue-Point Siamese queen with her litter of six kittens. This is quite a common number for the Siamese breeds, but through all breeds the size of a litter may vary from a single kitten to as many as a dozen. With very large litters it is wise to ask a vet's advice as to how many kittens the mother should be allowed to rear, for a large litter will put a great strain upon her.

Fortunately very few kittens come into the world at the cost of their mother's life, but it can sometimes happen and then the owner must be prepared to take full responsibility for its care. A tiny blind kitten, still literally damp behind the ears, is totally vulnerable and everything must be done for it. A suitable substitute for its mother's milk must be made up — cow's milk will *not* do — and feeds admistered every four hours, though after the first week it is possible to leave out the feed in the middle of the night. Milk can be given through a doll's bottle, but some pet shops stock special bottles made for the job. The best way of feeding is to place the kitten on your lap with a thick towel on your knees to give it something to grip on to. It is important to avoid draughts and extremes of temperature. The kitten's surroundings need to be kept at a temperature of about 32° Centigrade (90° Fahrenheit) for the first day, above 29° Centigrade (85° Fahrenheit) for the next four days and gradually level off to about 21° Centigrade (70° Fahrenheit) at the end of the fourth week. To wash them don't lick them — your tongue isn't like a cat's! — but use a coarse towel to replace it. Washing not only keeps them clean, it stimulates their internal organs and pushes food throught them. It will be much easier if you can find a foster mother with sufficient milk and energy to take on another kitten. Rubbing the kitten with a little milk from the foster mother, or with her urine, may help the cat to accept the orphan as her own. Feline mothers keep a watchful eye on kittens who stray too far from their nesting box or explore beyond a reasonable range. If they do not respond to a call or a little chivvying, the mother will pick them up and carry them back to base. In case of danger a cat will carry its whole litter, one by one, to a place of safety.

Top left
This Blue-Point Siamese is about to lift her kitten. She is placing her teeth gently about a loose fold of skin on the kitten's neck, gripping it firmly enough to hold the kitten but without doing any harm. The mother cat uses her teeth because she cannot use her paws, but humans should not pick cats up by the scruff of the neck alone. The proper way for humans to pick up a small kitten is to place the hand under the body, with the fingers under the neck supporting the head, so that the kitten is cradled in the palm. When it gets a little larger you can lift it gently by the neck, supporting its rear end with your other hand, or lift it with one hand under the body just behind the front paws and

the other supporting its hindquarters. Hold it in the crook of your arm or, supporting its hindquarters, allow it to hold on to you with its front paws. Children, in particular, should be taught how to handle kittens for they are often thoughtless in the way that they treat pets.
Some kittens will prefer to rest their paws on your shoulders and look at what is going on behind *above*, while others will delight in actually sitting on your shoulder — or even the top of your head — and going along for the ride.

Left
The cat tries to keep her head well up to

avoid bumping the kitten on the ground but as her kittens get older she will drag them along if it proves necessary. For some reason not yet understood, white kittens, sometimes deaf when they are young and their eyes are blue, are able to hear when their eyes change colour as they grow older. Adult all-white cats with blue eyes are usually deaf, and it has been claimed that odd-eyed cats with one blue eye are deaf in the ear on the side of the blue eye, though this has not been proved. If a white kitten has a dark smudge on its head between the ears, like the one being carried here, this is said to indicate good hearing even though the eyes stay blue and the smudge disappears as the kitten grows up.

Two different kinds of basket: *above* is one that gives some shelter from draughts, and *top right* a simple round basket. For bedding place layers of newspaper which are warm and cats find comfortable. A blanket on top will add extra luxury for kittens.

Right
This fellow knows what is expected of him. A kitten's mother will almost certainly have taught it clean habits but if there should be the occasional accident do not scold the kitten. If you are there when it happens simply pick the kitten up and carry it to its tray. If you are not there there is little you can do other than clean up the mess so that the smell does not make the kitten use the same place again.

Above and *right*
When your kitten is older it may appreciate a daily saucer of milk but do not be too worried if it does not. Some cats, particularly among the oriental breeds, do not like milk and because few cats can digest cow's milk properly, it may cause stomach upsets. If a growing kitten will not drink milk then an alternative source of calcium must be included in its diet to help it build strong bones. Even cats who will never touch milk put out for them will sometimes steal the cream from the top of an opened milk bottle, help themselves to milk from the milk jug or even lap up milk that has been spilt. Anything that was meant for someone else seems immediately to become desirable.

Left and *right*
Cats like a regular life and you should always try to keep to set meal times for feeding your kittens. For creatures with such small stomachs this will help to prevent over-eating and avoid indigestion. Nevertheless, cats are incorrigible thieves and a stolen titbit will always taste better than what is officially served. Even offered foodstuffs that are refused may then disappear from other plates, so try to avoid leaving food out as a temptation. As your kitten gets bigger, keep an eye open to be sure it has not learned to open the food store or the freezer — they sometimes do! If you don't think a cat should jump up on the table you must be firm about it when it is very small.

The variety of kittens

Which of the more than sixty breeds of cat is likely to be the right one for you? That depends upon what you think you want. The greatest difference between one breed and another lies in their physical appearance. They are all capable of being loving or vicious, thieves, casanovas, gourmets and psychopaths according to the way you treat them and the kind of influence you are. Some people think that orientals are more intelligent and more energetic — and they are certainly noisier in most cases. Others will claim that Persians are more affectionate. But there are plenty of neurotic long-hairs and not a few lazy Siamese. Orientals do tend to need more emotional attention and long-hairs must have more frequent grooming but a large part of that mixture of heredity and environment will be entirely up to you whether you choose a cat with an elaborate pedigree, or a cheeky faced kitten from some unrecorded random mating. If you give your cat love you will get love back, give it respect and it will respect you. Play the games it likes and it will agree to play your games too.

Individual breeders will have their own ideas about their own strains, and they know them best, but however good its stock a cat treated without consideration won't make a happy pet, and one that is overfed and never played with will grow fat and indolent however sophisticated its pedigree may be.

These pages
The Tabby is probably the best known of all types of cat and many household cats are tabby or part tabby in their make-up. Nevertheless the tabby breeds have to conform to strict standards like any other. The pattern appears in both long- and short-haired cats and through a number of colour variations. Blue, Brown, Cream and Red are all recognized breeds of long-hairs and Red, Brown, and Silver are the short-hair colours. In all cases the coat has a solid base colour with darker patterning and no white marks. The pattern can either be striped, known as 'mackerel', or in whorls, giving a butterfly-like marking on the shoulders and two chains on the chest. Tabby markings show at birth but sometimes

fade in the first few weeks, returning as the kittens grow older. The butterfly marks, according to one legend, show where the prophet Mahomet stroked the cat. Another version of the story says that it is the 'M' mark on the forehead which indicates where Mahomet gave his blessing. His fondness for cats is remembered in a legend which tells how he cut off the sleeve of his garment rather than disturb the favourite cat that had gone to sleep in it.

Following pages
Cats with luxurious silky fur like these Smoke, Tabby and Cameo kittens were once loosely known as Angora or Persian cats, but Angora is now the name of a specific breed and in Britain the term 'Persian' is no longer officially used. In America and elsewhere, however, it is still applied to the varieties of long-haired cats, and no doubt people will go on using it in this way. Long-haired cats originated in the east and were not known in Europe until the end of the 16th century.

Top left
A pair of sprightly Bi-coloured kittens.
Black and white and red and white
Bi-colours are recognized in both long-
haired and short-haired groups.

Left
If you are ignorant of the various breeds

of cat it will be difficult for you to imagine what many pedigree kittens will look like when they are adult, for they often change a great deal when they grow up. However, the Korat cat, or *Si-Sawat* as it is called in its native Siam, is a lovely silver blue from birth right through its life. Although Korat cats have been known in Thailand for centuries they have only recently been introduced to the West. They are probably more truly Siamese than the oriental breed that carries that name, although Siamese cats, too, have been established for a long time in Siam.

Above
All kittens are born with blue eyes, but at four to six weeks their eyes should have changed to their adult colour. If these kittens' eyes stay blue, or if they grow up with one eye blue and one orange, they will be classified into separate breeds from their orange-eyed mother.

Right
This cat and her kitten are known in Britain as Red Self long-hairs, and in the United States as Solid Reds or Red Persians. This is a difficult breed to produce and it is not yet possible to breed like-to-like because there are few females. The kitten has a fine even coat but tabby markings are sometimes prominent and do not fade until the cat has reached adulthood.

Left
A Long-haired Cream kitten. When it is older its blue eyes will change to orange.

Below left
A Long-haired Smoke kitten, already old enough to show the adult coat. The delicate colour effect is created by a white undercoat and a black topcoat which shades to silver on the sides and leaves a silver ruff and ear tufts. The undercoat shows clearly as the cat moves. A Blue Smoke is also recognized, and in America, Smoke is recognized as a colour variety of other kinds of cat.

Right
A beautiful Chinchilla mother and kitten, often called Silver in America. The undercoat is pure white with black or silver tipping on the ends of the fur of the back, flanks, head, ears and tail which gives it the characteristic sparkling appearance. Sometimes kittens show tabby markings indicative of the origins of the breed. The English breed is stockier than that favoured in America, but both have the enormous, round, emerald or blue-green eyes circled by dark rims.

Below
A British Blue kitten has the characteristic plush-like short hair of its breed, but a body conformation similar to that of the long-haired varieties. In France a very similar breed is known as the Chartreuse, and in shows the two are now treated as the same breed.

All the breeds illustrated here are of the long-haired Persian type with cobby bodies, short legs and round faces. Their fine coats require a lot of attention and must be brushed and combed at least once a day, if not more frequently.

Left
A proud Manx father with his kitten. A true Manx has no tail at all, but a large proportion of Manx litters have tails or stumps. They are not, therefore, eligible for showing, though a small tuft of fur is acceptable if it contains no bone or cartilage. Manx cats have a double coat and high rear quarters which give them a rabbity gait. They can be any colour provided the eye colour is in accordance with the coat.

Below
A Brown Burmese kitten. At first thought to be a very dark Siamese, this breed was discovered when a cat taken from Burma to the United States was found to be a hybrid of a Siamese and a previously unknown dark-coated breed. Its kittens were a mixture of pure Siamese and the darker-coated cats, which later proved to breed true.

Right
The Abyssinian cat is thought to resemble some of the cats of ancient Egypt. Its appearance suggests that it has close links with the wild cats of Africa, although others claim it is an entirely modern creation. The kittens are often born with dark coats and bars on the front legs, but these disappear as they grow older.
Every cat in Egypt was a sacred animal and rigorously protected by the religious law. It was particularly venerated as the symbol of the goddess Bast and was the form in which she was usually represented. It is easy to see why a kitten as beautiful as this should be held sacred to a goddess.

Left
A trio of playful Blue Burmese kittens. The Blue Burmese is a fairly recent development from the Brown Burmese and, though recognized by the British Cat Fancy in 1960, it has not yet been recognized by all the American societies.

Below and right
There are now six recognized breeds of Siamese cat: Seal Point, Chocolate Point, Blue Point, Lilac Point, Tabby Point (also known as Lynx Point), Red Point and Tortie Point. Siamese kittens start off fluffy and white with no sign of the darker points of the adult cat. The first sign of colour in their fur is a smudge of darker tint around the nose. The experienced breeder can recognize their breed from the nose leather and paw pads which will be black for a Seal Point, brown for a Chocolate, grey for a Blue and grey nose leather with pinkish pads for a Lilac. Even as kittens they have longer and more tapering tails than domestic cats of the West. Often their tails used to have a kink, and although this is now considered a fault in show cats, it gave rise to many charming legends. One tells of a Siamese cat who was set to guard a sacred chalice. Fearful lest he fall asleep he curled his tail around the stem of the holy cup so that it should be secure and none should take it from him. He was at his post for so long before he was relieved that his tail was permanently bent but he carried it proudly as proof of his faith and fortitude.

Below a Tabby Point family, sometimes known as Lynx Point.
Top, a Blue Point kitten and *below* a Lilac Point mother and kitten.

The graceful body, elegant markings and beautiful almond eyes of Siamese cats were already well established in the cats of the royal palace in Siam more than 150 years ago. They are said to have played a curious role in royal funerals. When a prince of the royal house died, one of his cats was put into the tomb with him. A small hole was left in the roof of the vault and through this the cat would eventually escape. The watching priests would then know that the soul of the dead prince had passed into the cat and ascended from the tomb. Siamese kittens are great conversationalists and will enjoy having lengthy chats with their humans. As the Siamese kitten grows older, the baby squeaks and cheeps gradually become the loud and distinctive voice which is characteristic of the breed.

Below Seal Point kittens.

Right A pair of kittens photographed in California.

Black cats used to be thought the agents
of the devil, perhaps because cats were
venerated in pagan faiths and because the
devil was the Prince of Darkness. In
America a black cat is still considered to
be unlucky, but the opposite is true in
England, where if a black kitten rubs
against your legs it is a sign of great good
luck to come.

Far left
This might seem to be a Siamese kitten in
need of a haircut . . . however, a second
glance will show you that although it has
the characteristic Siamese points, this

kitten does not have a pointed oriental
head but the broad round head, smaller
ears and cobby body of a Persian cat. It is
a Himalayan kitten, or Colourpoint, as it
is called in Britain. Similar cats have been
bred by accident, but the Colourpoint
breed has been carefully created to
combine the coat and conformation of
the Persian type with the marking of the
Siamese. They may be Seal Point like this
kitten or any other of the Siamese
colours.

Above
A Spotted kitten, a British short-haired
type, is comparatively rare among

pedigreed cats, although the type can be
seen in Egyptian paintings and Pompeian
mosaics. They were once known as
Spotted Tabbies, but since tabby has
always been taken to mean striped, the
Breed Standard has been amended. The
spots need not necessarily be round but
they should not be long and narrow so
that they look like a broken stripe. Any
colour is permitted.

Left
A Red Colourpoint kitten. Blue, Lilac,
Chocolate and Tortie Points have also
been bred.

Below
This Tortoiseshell and White cat, known as a Calico in some sections of the American Cat Fancy, has a litter of mixed colour kittens. Only one takes after its mother, and that is almost certainly female. This beautiful colouring rarely occurs in a male cat, and when it does the cat is almost invariably sterile so that it is impossible to breed like to like.

Below right
A Birman cat and kitten. As in the Siamese, the kitten's 'points' will spread and darken to become like those of the adult cat. This breed has been popular in France for many years but has only recently become known in Britain and America. It comes from Burma and Cambodia in Southeast Asia, and

although, like the Colourpoint, it looks at first glance like a Siamese with long hair, it has very individual characteristics. The head is round and slightly flattened on top. Full cheeks, stocky legs and a well-bushed tail give the adult a totally different look from the Siamese. On close inspection you will find that the points are also different — in particular the Birman has white feet. In Britain Seal and Blue varieties are recognized but Chocolate and Lilac can also be shown in the United States. The Birman is also known as the Sacred Cat of Burma, and legend has it that it was originally a white cat at the Temple of Lao-Tsun. Here it would join the chief priest in the worship of the blue-eyed, golden goddess Tsun-Kyan-Kse. One night when the priests were gathered in the temple asking

the goddess for guidance and protection from a threatened foreign invasion, the chief priest died. As the old man's body failed him, the cat leaped upon his head. The watching priests saw its fur change to the gold of the goddess and its eyes to sapphire blue, while its ears and paws became the colour of fertile earth except for where they rested on the old man's silver head. The priests then knew that the spirit of the old man had passed into the cat. They saw the cat turn from the goddess and face the outer door of the temple, beyond which the sound of approaching soldiers could be heard. Given courage by the strength now invested in the cat, the priests repelled every attack and saved the temple. For seven days the cat sat gazing at the goddess, and then it died, taking the spirit

of the old priest with it. When the priests gathered to choose a successor, they found one of their number surrounded by all the other cats of the temple, who had now also taken on the golden colour and blue eyes of the goddess, and they knew that he was destined to be their new chief priest.

Right
The Van Cat, known in Britain as the Turkish Cat, comes from the Lake Van area of southeastern Turkey where it has been prized for centuries. Van Cats were introduced to Britain in the mid 1950s and recognized as a breed in 1969. They actively enjoy water (see page 53).

Above
A Foreign White kitten, a recently
recognized breed which is a Siamese cat
with no points. A dominant gene
produces the white coat, although it also
carries the genetic information for
coloured points.

Left
This kitten stretching itself is a Red-Point
Siamese with the curly coat of Rex fur.
Its mother was a Siamese and its father a
Rex-furred tabby. The Rex type, of
which there are two varieties, developed
from a mutant form produced by chance
in the west of England. It now breeds
true, however, and the Cornish and
Devon types are considered separate
breeds.

Right
The Foreign Lavender, or Foreign Lilac,
is a Siamese type cat with a self colour
coat. It is difficult to breed, for both
parents must carry both blue and
chocolate genes and like-to-like breeding
has only recently been established. In this
litter only one of the kittens carries its
mother's colour; the others will be Lilac
Siamese. The breed has already received
recognition from some American
societies.

Discovery and exploration

Below
All kittens are inquisitive, but by the time they are old enough to leave their mothers they should have learned to be cautious too. Like this tabby, they will always prefer to carry out an initial reconnaissance from behind cover, sizing up not only the danger presented by the new object or new terrain, but also their own line of retreat. If something does not move after a reasonable period, which will get longer as the kitten gets older and grows in patience, they will venture out for a closer scrutiny. If there is any doubt about an object, a tap with a forepaw often followed by a rapid retreat and further close scrutiny, will establish whether it moves or is, in fact, inanimate.

Right
Next comes a careful sniffing out for further information, like the investigation this Abyssinian kitten is making. If the scent is particularly enjoyable or intriguing, or needs intensification, the kitten will open its mouth to increase its sensitivity to smell. When it is confident that there is no danger and its curiosity is satisfied, it will very likely sit down and wash.

Below right
If you take your kitten to a new or strange house let it investigate the new surroundings in its own time. When it settles down and begins to wash you will know that it has accepted its new or temporary home. A cat can reach every part of its body with its tongue except the head, the back of the neck and between the shoulder blades. It uses its tongue as sponge, brush and comb — and even towel if it gets accidently wet! To reach inaccessible places it moistens its paws and scrubs with them.

Left
A well-trained kitten will tread warily if there is chance of harm and will keep a watchful eye for any danger but the occasional fright or minor scratch are a small price to pay for the pleasure of it all and the opportunity to lead a more natural life will make for a less neurotic cat. *Centre* Ever cautious, this little tabby whips round trying to identify the noise it thinks it heard.

Below
These two tabby kittens setting out on safari are concentrating all their highly developed senses. Their ears, which can register a range of more than 30,000 cycles per second, are shaped and lined with ridges to collect the sound. They can be moved forward, backward, up and down, while their necks are so flexible that they can be turned to locate a sound from any direction. Cats have extremely sensitive sight, and in hunting rely on this rather than on smell — the only mammals, apart from man and monkeys, to do so. Their angle of view is over 200°; their pupils can open very wide or narrow to a tiny slit, allowing vision in a wide range of light conditions; and they can focus very rapidly. Reflecting cells at the back of the retina increase the sensitivity so that they can see when we find ourselves in apparent darkness. An extra eyelid, the nictitating membrane, can fold over the eye from the lower inner corner to give added protection from very bright light, injury in a fight or prickly under-growth. The whole of a kitten's body is extremely sensitive to touch, and pressure on a single hair will immediately send a message to the brain. Both the whiskers and the long hairs on the back of the forepaws respond not only to direct contact but also to changes in air pressure caused by the proximity or movement of objects. Smell, which plays a smaller role, is used only at short distances for precise location when sight has already established general location. It plays a major role in the sex life of the adult cat, however, and smell sensations obviously give kittens great pleasure.

Right
Has the attention of this pair of white and tabby kittens been attracted by a bug climbing up the stalk, or have they just imagined it? Cats become very adept at catching insects. Keeping your kitten indoors will not remove the risk of infection, for you are very likely to bring in germs yourself on your clothes and on your shoes. However, if you live in an area of heavy traffic or where un-neutered toms instigate a lot of fights, you may feel the risks could become too great. If you do keep your cat indoors you must compensate by giving up much more time to playing games, even if you have two animals to keep each other company.

Above
Body compact, paws extended and nose down, this kitten waits for the moment to release its concentrated energy in a spring. Its eyes are focused on the prey, watching unblinkingly for the moment of attack. Just before making the spring it will probably wiggle its hindquarters. Most cats do this, perhaps to distract the quarry, much as lions are believed to wave the feathery tip on the end of their tails. In an older cat the ears would be pressed down and back to make it less noticeable.

Right
When hunting, whether as a game or in deadly earnest, a kitten learns to use all available cover and to concentrate its energies for a final spring.
This Tortoiseshell and White has remembered to keep low and is using the vegetation and the unevenness of the ground to hide him, but he has not yet learned to keep his ears back and out of sight.

Left
Moving cautiously, body extended and as close to the ground as possible, an Abyssinian kitten focuses ears and eyes on the movements of its prey but keeps its head set low to avoid detection.

Previous page
Animals that are reared together, like this dachshund and litter of Russian Blues, are more aware of their kinship than their differences and will make happy play-mates — but they will probably treat outside cats and dogs with the suspicion and hostility that is traditional.

Left
Two small kittens greet each other and exchange an investigation by nose to see what the other has been up to. Notice how your own cat investigates where you have been and whom you have met when next you return from a trip outside the house. They will identify all the smell contacts you have picked up as though you were recounting your excursion to them.

Most kittens are delighted to make friends with other animals. If another creature approaches a kitten quietly and calmly, its interest will soon overcome its fear, but if a barking, bouncing puppy rushes at the kitten it will probably be mistaken for an attacker and the kitten will beat a hasty retreat.

Left
The guinea pig is unmoved by the white kitten's presence, but the kitten is unsure whether this is a potential playmate or something which just might bite.

Right
A snail is rather baffling. 'How can *anyone* move so slowly?' this bemused kitten asks.

Below
This Lilac Point Siamese is very wary of the goat and has adopted an aggressive posture. This is a clear warning that there is to be no nonsense, and it is taken in the hope that a show of power will intimidate any would-be aggressor. Unfortunately this aggressive presentation as a form of defence can sometimes be taken as a real threat and lead to trouble.

Right
A kitten which has never met a puppy before shows all the signs of fear. The fur stands on end and the tail in particular bushes out, making the kitten, it hopes, a much bigger and more terrifying opponent for any aggressor.

Far right
French peasants in the middle ages thought that farmyard cats that slept all day did so in order to be alert all night to keep watch on the devil's behalf and warn the evil spirits they could hear chattering in the straw of the approach of any good man or holy thing. With that sort of belief it is not surprising that many an old lady keeping a pet kitten for company was suspected of being a witch and the cat of being her 'familiar'.

Left

The old proverb that a cat likes fish but doesn't like to get its feet wet is not always true for most cats and kittens are fascinated by running water. A cat will spend hours watching a tap drip, sometimes trying to catch the drops on its tongue, sometimes tentatively catching them on an outstretched paw which is then shaken to throw the wetness off. Many cats will dip a paw into a jug to pick up milk too deep for their tongue to reach, but few like any liquid falling on them. The fish in this garden pool are tempting and his owners have wisely arranged netting around its edge to thwart the kitten's intentions. There are many authenticated cases of angling cats: W. H. Hudson wrote of a cat which caught a daily trout for dinner. Most cats scoop the fish out of shallow water with a paw — this is how wildcats catch fish along the Scottish seashore — but some are said to angle by tapping the surface of the water with their tails to attract the fish, as jaguars are believed to do in South America.

Below left

Not many cats actually choose to swim, although domestic cats will swim instinctively if they have to. The hunting cats seen in ancient Egyptian paintings presumably swam to retrieve shot fowl. Wildcats are known to swim, but this kitten belongs to the only recognized domestic breed which regularly enjoys taking to the water. It is a Van Cat, seen here in a Turkish river.

Top right

If your kitten is allowed to go outdoors it will be able to indulge in a whole world of new sensual experiences only guessed at from the other side of the window pane. These three kittens exploring in their garden can enjoy the excitement that comes with the feel of the fresh air, the scurry of leaves on the lawn, the slight rustle of another animal among the flowers. There are trees to climb, walls to scale, trunks to exercise claws on, bark to scratch the back on, paving and concrete to roll on, insects to catch, other animals to meet and hundreds of new smells to savour are carried on the breeze or lie strong and pungent on the earth: it is all new and different.

Right

Evening, the cat's natural hunting time, is when his sharp eyes and carefully attuned hearing really come into their own. Look at the way this kitten has his ears finely focused to locate the source of a sound that has particularly caught his attention.

In high places

Right
All cats like to look down on the world. A wall provides a refuge from a troublesome dog, though this Siamese does not seem convinced it is foolproof.

Right
Kittens find step-ladders irresistible too. If you are doing any painting, watch out for a curious kitten. Not only can you find your paint pots flying, but you may end up with a paint-covered cat. If you do, wipe off as much paint as you can and get the kitten to the vet. Paint solvents and detergents can do serious damage to a cat's skin and some kinds of paint may themselves be poisonous.

Left
Even a toy tractor seat is a vantage point if there is nothing higher about, but not sufficient to hold the attention where there is a game of follow-my-leader going on. Despite their fluffy appearance these are short-haired white kittens. It was probably a cat of this type that an Irish monk shared his cell with long ago. He wrote a poem about it:

> *'I and Pangur Ban, my cat,*
> *'Tis a like task we are at;*
> *Hunting mice is his delight,*
> *Hunting words I sit all night.'*

White cats are considered lucky in America, and if you believe old rhymes and have a weight problem you will be glad to know the following:

> *'Kiss the black cat*
> *An 'twill make ye fat,*
> *Kiss the white ane,*
> *'Twill make ye lean.*

Cats love climbing trees, but kittens often find that having got up they cannot get down. Having made it to the topmost branches, this tabby *above* must be wondering why what seemed so easy on the way up could look so daunting in the opposite direction.

Left
A young Siamese makes a rapid descent: has it just heard that dinner is ready or has someone suggested he join in a more stimulating game? Instead of jumping straight from a branch it is virtually 'running' down the trunk. Whether jumping up or down, cats seem to be able to take a step or two on a vertical surface without difficulty, sometimes almost making a double leap to climb a wall.

Top right
This kitten seems full of confidence but even the cleverest cats can get into difficulties. If your kitten wears a collar, make sure that it will stretch sufficiently to enable the kitten to pull its head through should it get caught up on a twig. Otherwise you may find your pet unnecessarily 'treed'.

Right
This Long-haired Red seems very unsure of whether it ought to go any higher.

Kittens at play

Below
Kittens endow all their games with a vivid imagination but an imaginary opponent is not nearly so much fun as a real play-mate. Little kittens are rarely vicious, and a lively rough-and-tumble will do no one any harm. When they grow up, however – particularly if unneutered and allowed out on the prowl – a fight may have more serious consequences. A cat's flesh heals very quickly, but if a bite or scratch heals over dirt, it may lead to an abscess and require veterinary treatment.

Right
Kittens, and grown cats too, are especially delighted when a human friend pulls a piece of string for them to chase: following it over obstacles, around corners, behind furniture, through bushes or between legs provides a greater element of surprise. Sometimes they will chase after the tail, but frequently they will crouch, eyes fixed on the spot where the string is disappearing, delaying their pounce until the very last moment.

Right
With a table-tennis ball trapped between its forepaws a tabby kitten brings up its hindlegs to give it a savage battering. This is a typical fighting technique if the opponent can be held down.

Below
Open out the pages of a newspaper on the floor and lay them across each other with the centre folds peaked up like tents so that there is space between the layers. Now wait for your kitten to attack. Each hump hides a separate enemy, each rustle as the paper settles indicates a hidden opponent, and once inside, it makes ideal cover from which to prepare an assault on an unsuspecting victim. The crackle of paper gives it an added interest for kittens, for they can locate it with their sensitive ears as well as with their eyes. Siamese and other cats which delight in retrieving games often prefer a lightly crumpled paper ball, for it can still be heard even after it has landed and is easy to pick up in the teeth.

Above
An alabaster egg is an exciting discovery for this long-haired kitten, and it is delicately testing to see just how much of a push will make it move. The egg is unlikely to remain on the desk for long.

Top left
Does this kitten simply see a moving piece of string or has it become in his imagination a sinuously gliding serpent? Snakes seem to have a particular fascination for cats, although they rarely eat them, and in ancient mythology cats and snakes were often linked as symbolic adversaries. It is in the shape of a cat that the ancient Egyptians visualized their sun god Ra when he daily overcame the serpent Apep, who represented the darkness of the night.

Left
A resilient table-tennis ball is light enough to be moved with only a very small tap, and on hard surfaces can be made to bounce. Because of this it will change direction frequently, making it more interesting to chase. Here a tortoiseshell and white kitten has trapped a table-tennis ball between its paws. Many cats become extremely dexterous, not only at catching, but also lifting things between their forepaws.

Right
Kittens like all kinds of toys and use them, just as children do, to investigate and test their own abilities and to simulate the situations they will have to face as independent adults. A piece of string or a ball of wool makes a very versatile toy. Even on its own it provides a tunnel to investigate if you are as small as this short-haired Blue. Dangling in the air it forms a moving target to jump at. Tie a weight on the end, such as a cotton reel, and it can be strung up for a kitten to play with on its own.

Left
A pair of kittens give each other company and fun all the time and rely less upon their owner.

A ball on a piece of string offers endless possibilities. The fretted surface of this plastic ball makes it easier to grip than a smooth table-tennis ball. Hitting the ball will make the string trail out behind like an express worm and jerking the string will set the ball in motion. A little armchair speculation makes it clear how one leads to the other—and when the interest palls you can always ask a friend to join in the game (*over*).

Kittens put so much energy into every minute of their waking hours that they soon tire themselves. In the middle of a game they will suddenly nod off; indeed they spend a great part of their young lives asleep. A little later they will wake with a yawn and a stretch and rush off again into non-stop play.

Below
'Of course I'm not tired. And I wasn't yawning! I just thought that you might like to see what sharp teeth and a healthy tongue I have.' But, bleary-eyed and only just emerging from a blanket of deep sleep, it takes a moment or two for a kitten to pull itself together — although if danger threatens it is amazing how quickly those reactions can be speeded up. Like humans, cats can either sleep very superficially so they are wakened by the slightest sound, or go into a really deep sleep from which only a major disturbance will wake them.

Acknowledgements

The publishers would like to thank the following individuals and organizations for their kind permission to reproduce the pictures in this book:—

Bavaria-Verlag 24 top, 45, 55 top, 60 right S. C. Bisserot 6 bottom left Camera Press 5, 6 right, 42, 61 top, 71 Colour Library International 9 centre, 28-29 Anne Cumbers 16, 17 top, centre, bottom, 20 top, 30 bottom, 32 bottom, 32 top right, 33 top, 33 bottom, 36 top, 36 bottom, 40 top right, 41, 43 bottom, 44 top, 50 bottom C. M. Dixon 7 Susan Griggs 57 bottom Sonia Halliday 43 top, 56 bottom Louise Hughes 39, 63 Jane Miller 55 top right, 66 centre John Moss 9 top, 23 bottom, 25 top, 25 bottom, 47 top, 47 bottom, 64 top, 64-65, top Natural History Photographic Agency/Stephen Dalton 46 Peter Smith 66 top right, 67 Spectrum Colour Library 6 top left, 10, 13 top, 19, 21, 48 top, 48 centre, 50 top, 54 bottom, 56 top, 57 top, 59 bottom, 68 top, centre, bottom, 69, 70, 72 Tony Stone Associates 8, 9 bottom, 14-15, 30 top, 30-31, 32 top, 49, 51, 52-53 Sally Anne Thompson 2-3, 11, 13 bottom, 18, 20 bottom, 22, 23 top, 24 bottom, 26, 27 top, 27 bottom, 34 top, 35, 37 top, 37 bottom, 38, 40 top, 40 bottom left, 44 bottom, 48 bottom, 54 top, 54 centre, 55 bottom left, 58, 61 bottom